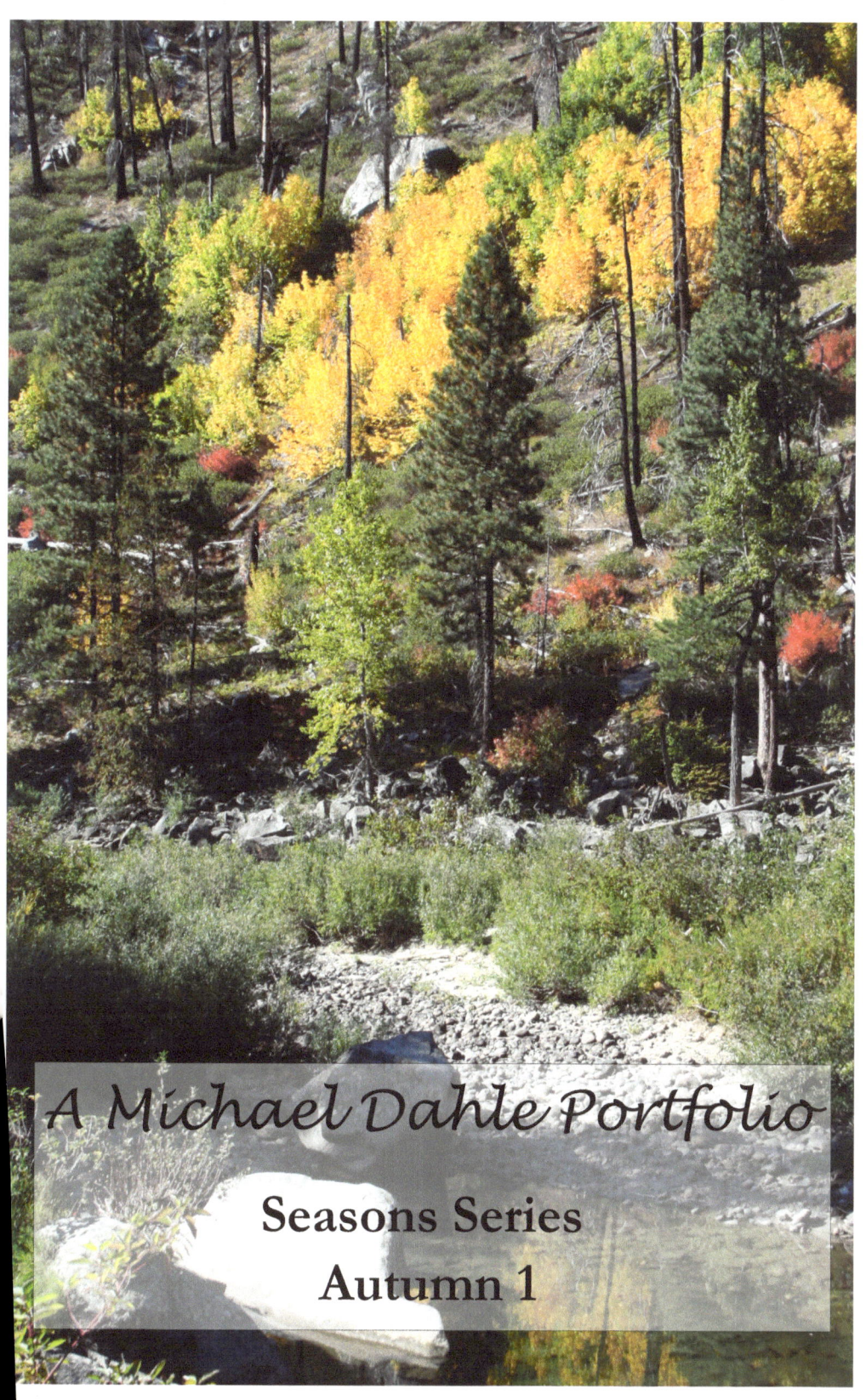

A Michael Dahle Portfolio

Seasons Series

Autumn 1

A MICHAEL DAHLE PORTFOLIO

This multi-book portfolio features photographs and writings by Michael Dahle.

Michael Dahle's photographic images are also available in products such as apparel, mugs, and tote bags; as limited edition enlargements for decorating your home or business; and for commercial use.

For more information visit MichaelDahle.com.

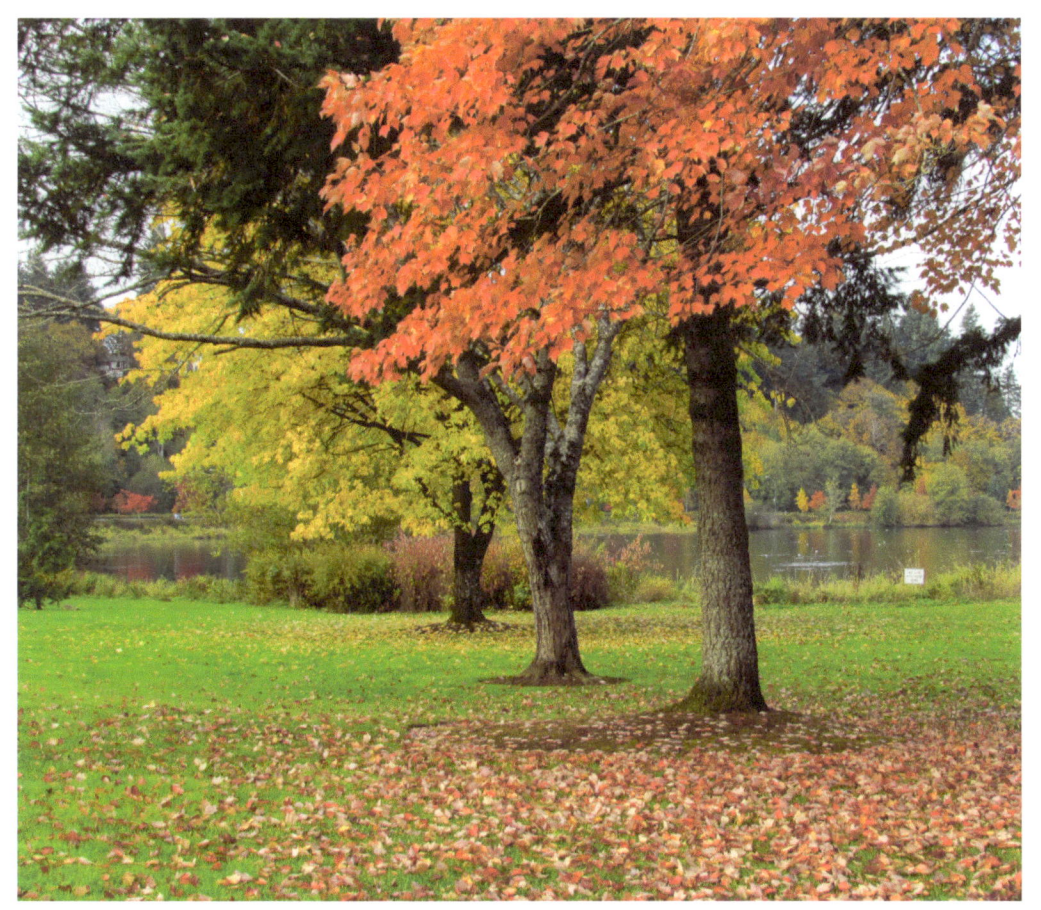

SEASONS SERIES

AUTUMN 1

The primary focus of the Michael Dahle Portfolio series is the presentation of Michael Dahle's photographs for your enjoyment. A secondary focus is to present Michael Dahle's writings.

In this book you will find photographs, poetry and writings by Michael Dahle as well as some facts about Autumn.

FACTS

In the Northern hemisphere Autumn, also called Fall, is roughly from September 21 through December 21.

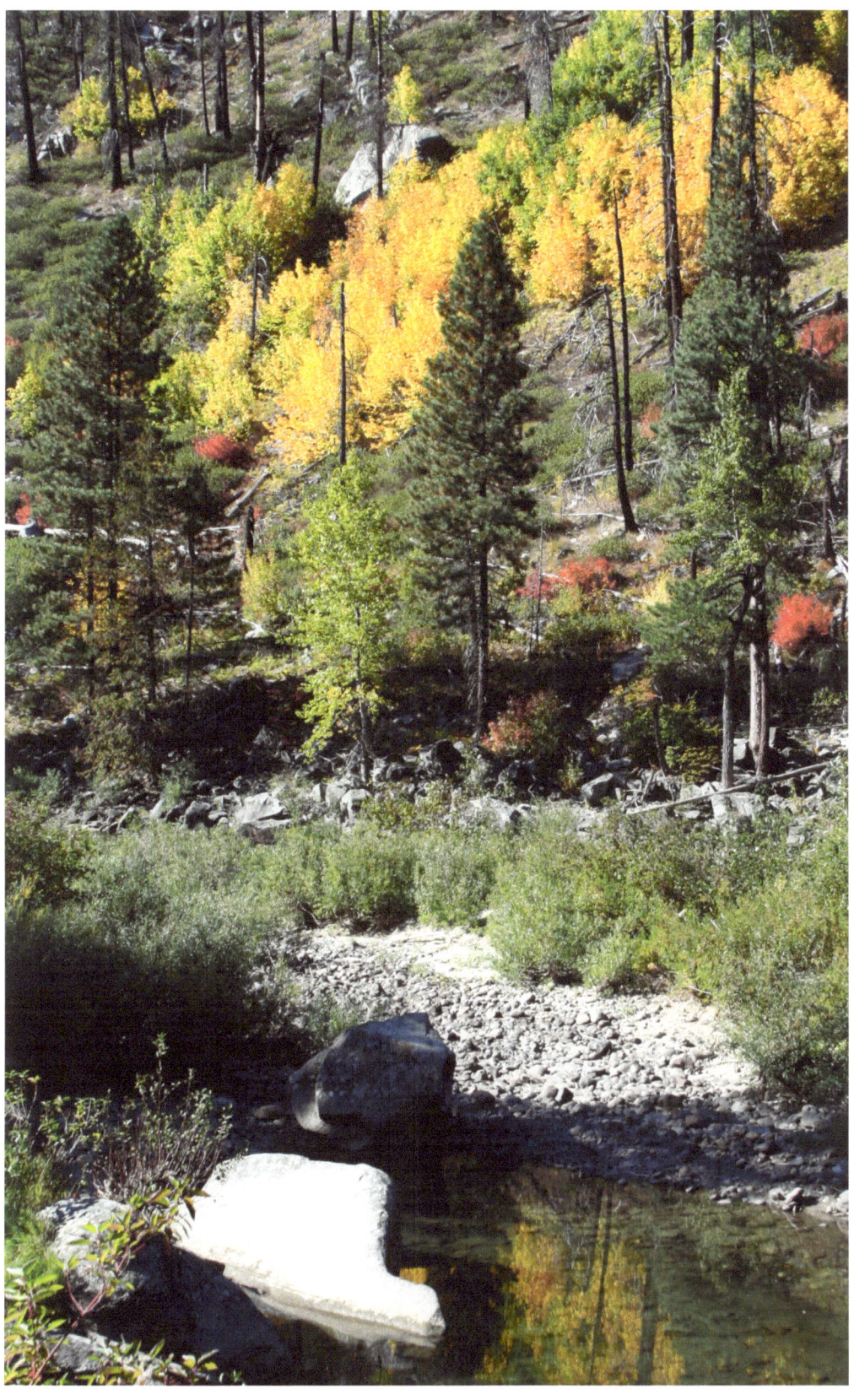

AUTUMN

Amazing colors
Underfoot crunching
Trees shedding
Unique scents
Mingled emotions
Nights cooling

Facing Page: Wenatchee River, Washington

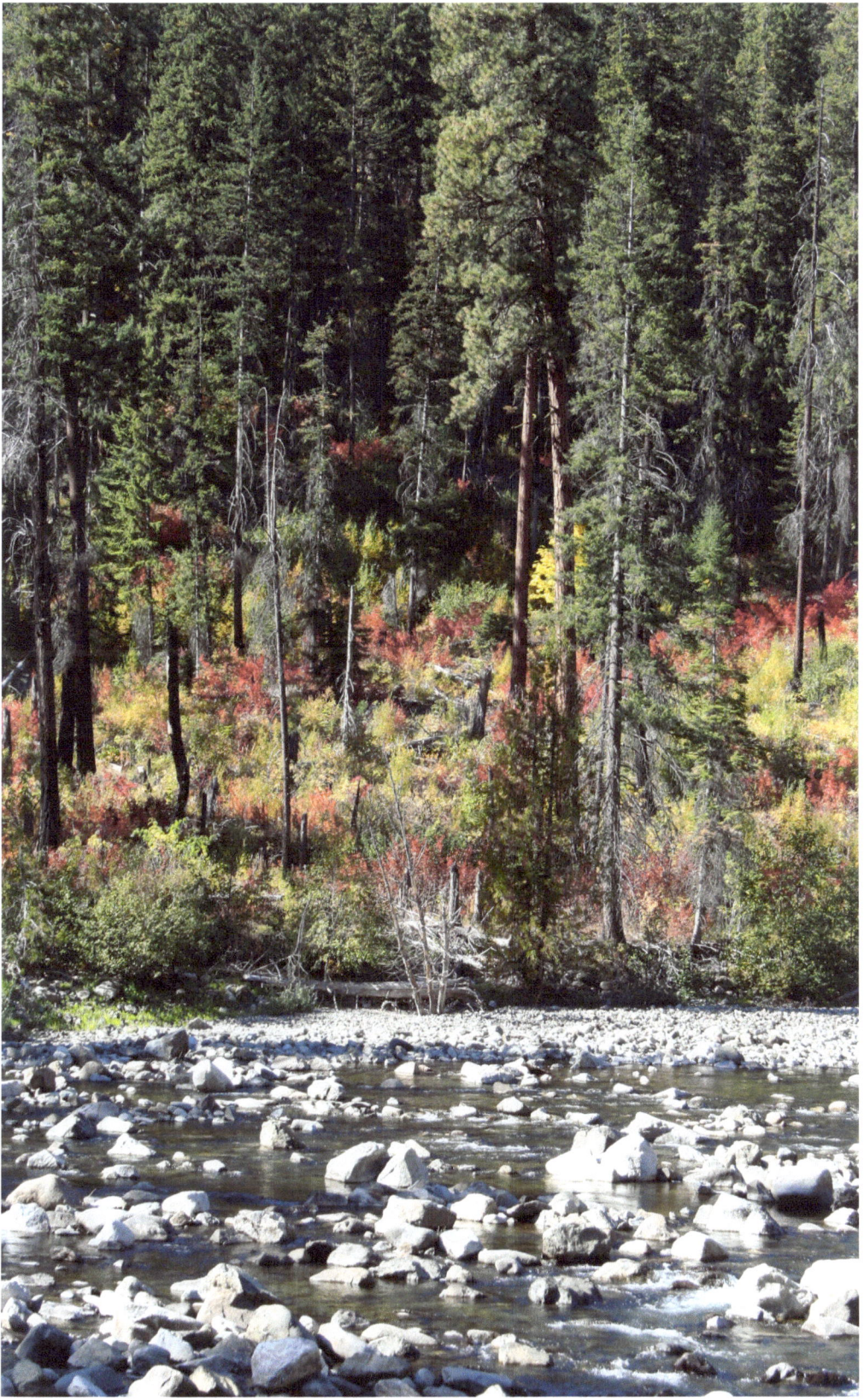

<u>THOUGHTS</u>

Autumn is a time of:
Color
Change
Inner beauty emerging
Special aromas

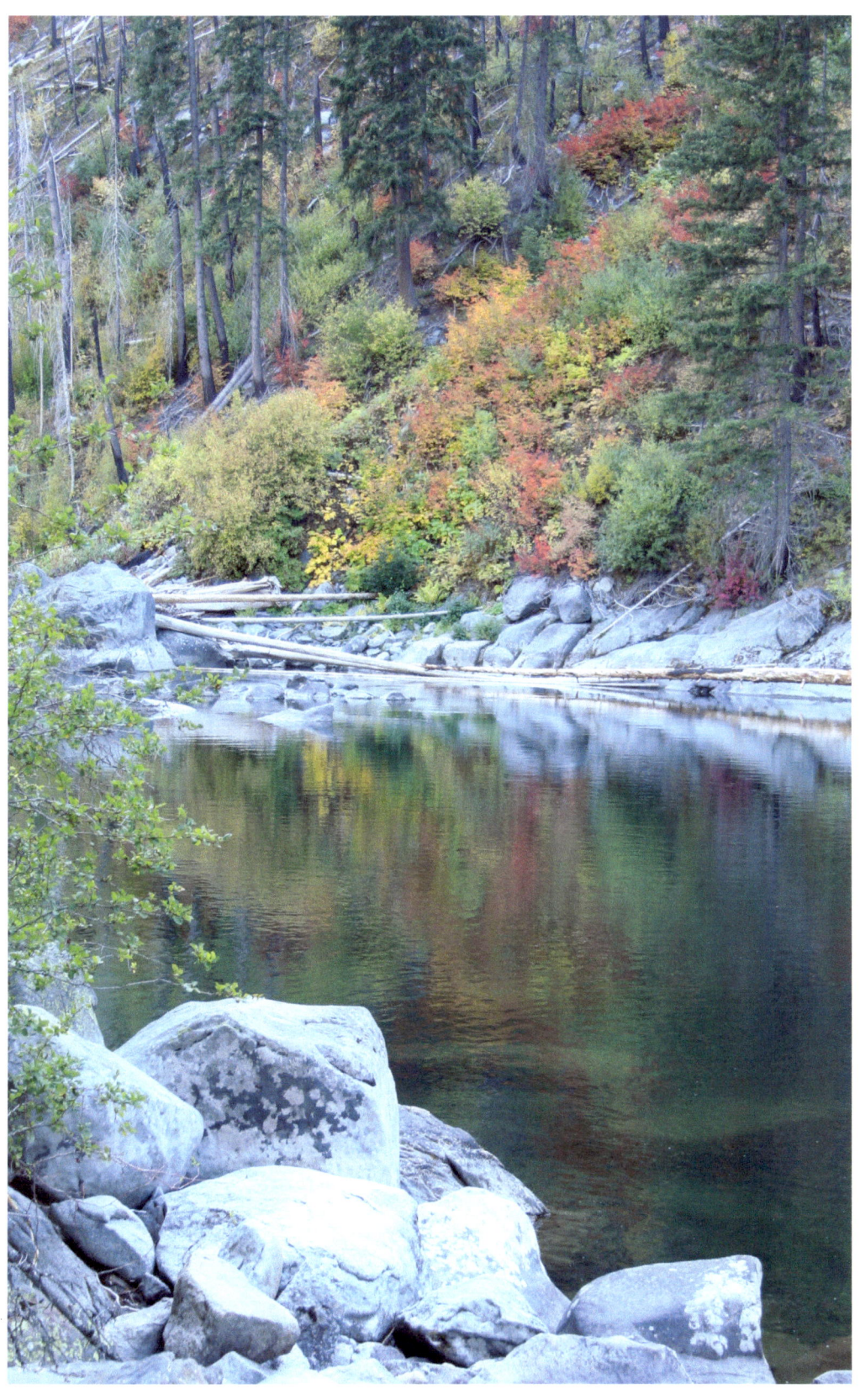

A FRIEND - A WALK

A friend and I,
For a walk went,
On a crisp afternoon,
Meandering along the river,
Autumn colors to see.

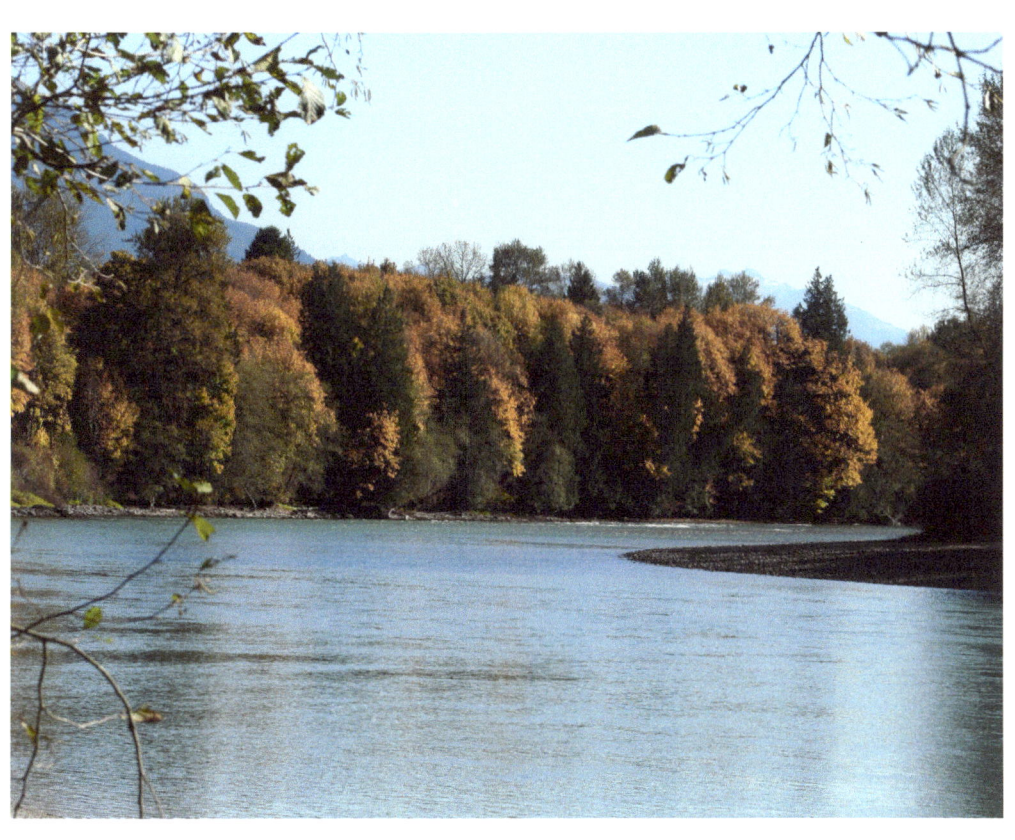

AUTUMN SENSES

Breath deep the cool crisp air,
Savor the warmth of late season sun,
Gaze upon the blue skies so fair,
Crunch through the leaves for fun,
Soak in the multi-colored flair.

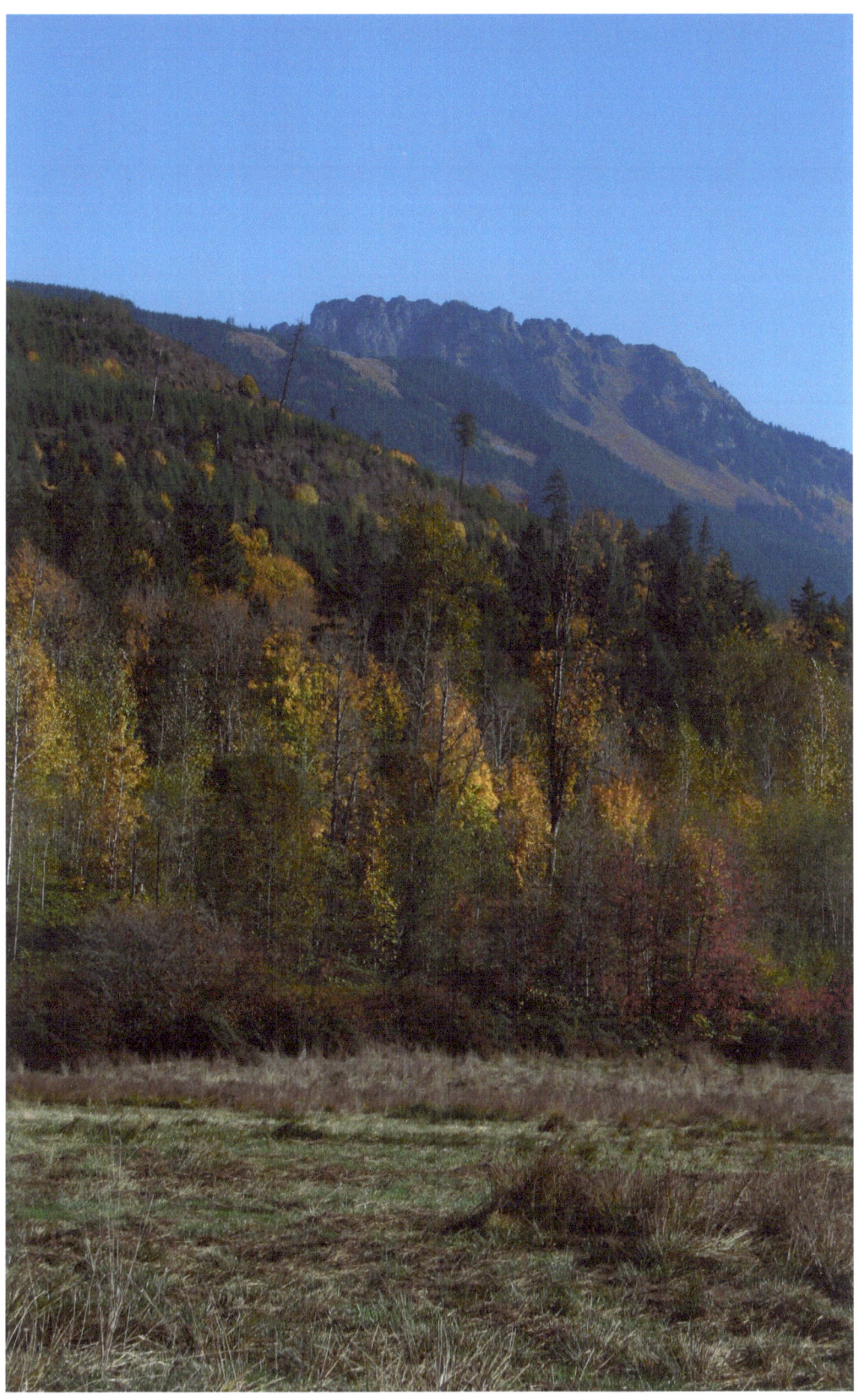

FACTS

Some of the trees that give us spectacular Autumn colors are:
Maples
Oaks
Elms
Birch
Ash
Bald Cypress
Aspen
Sourwood
Sweetgum
Dogwood
Ginkgo

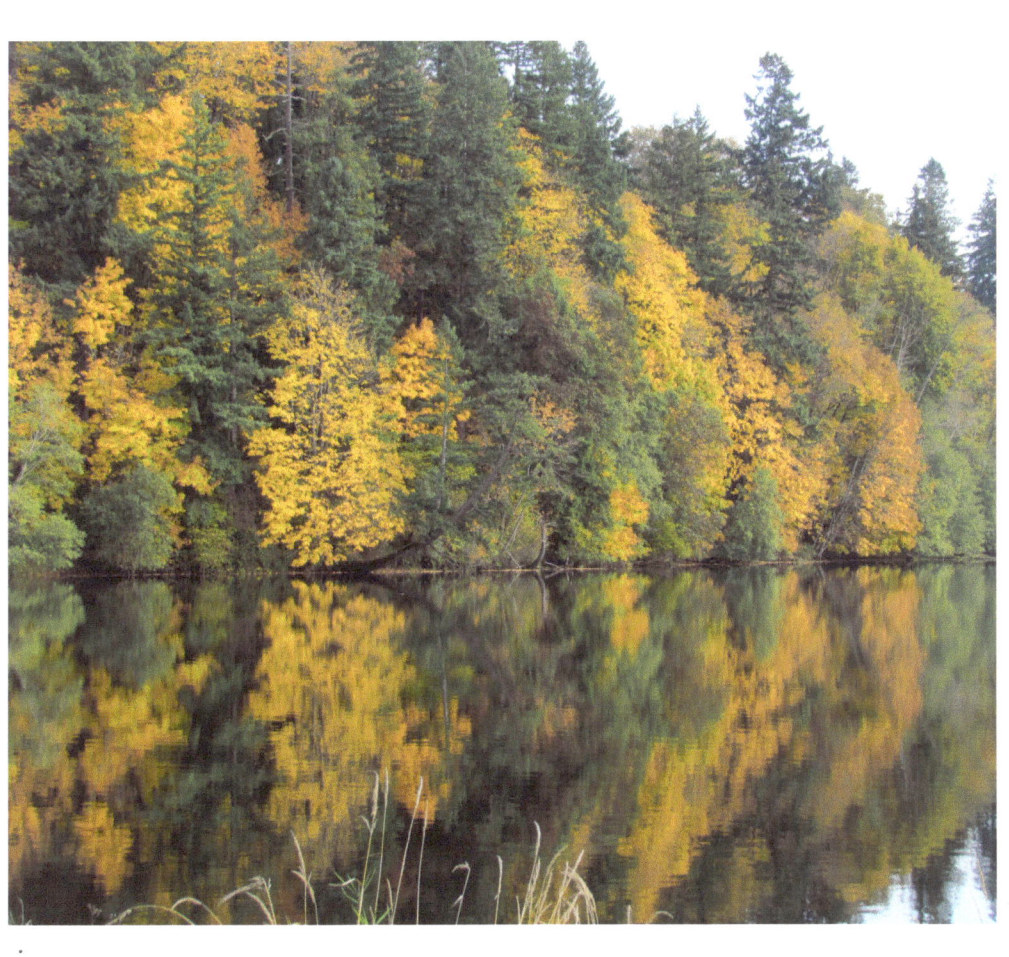

COLORS BRIGHT

Autumn colors bright
Yellows reds of many hues
My senses delight

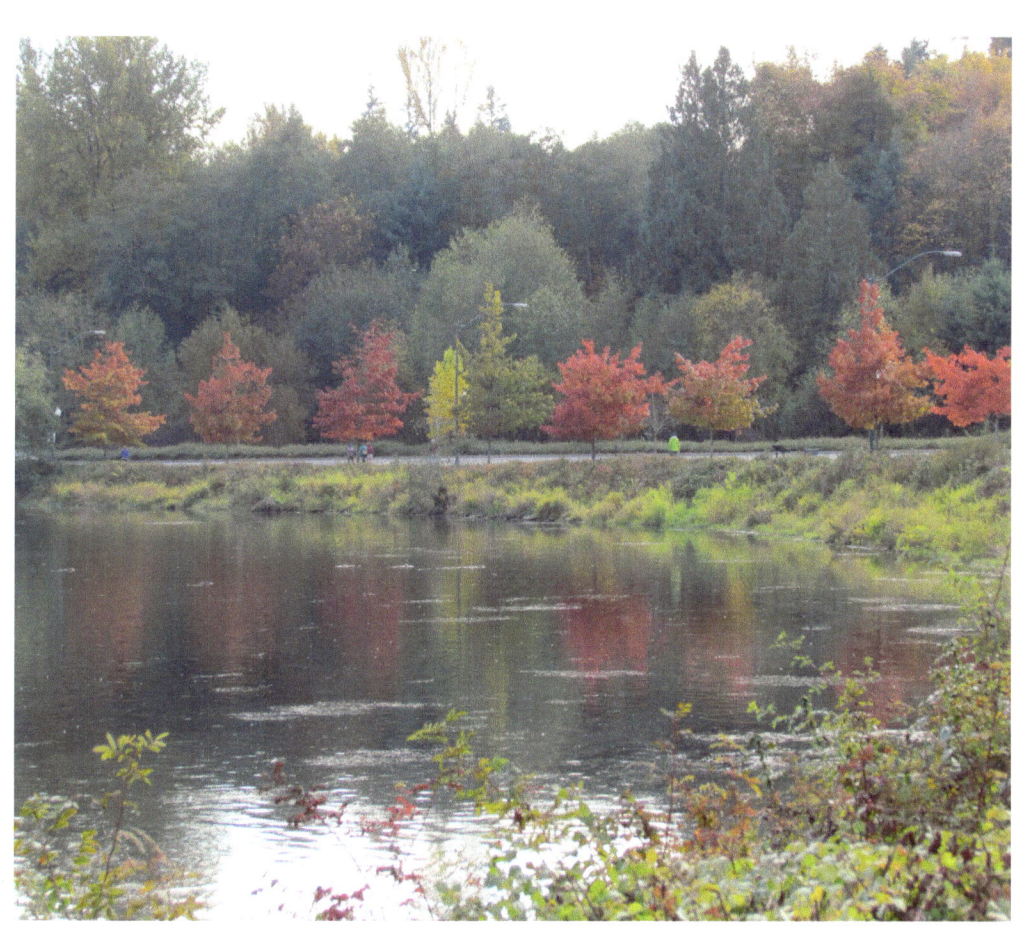

FACTS

Some of the shrubs that bring us spectacular Autumn colors are:
Chokeberry
Sumac
Witch Hazel
Viburnum
Serviceberry
Virginia Sweetspire
Hydrangea
Redbud
Burning Bush
Smoke Bush
Pomegranate
Blueberry
Red-Twig Dogwood

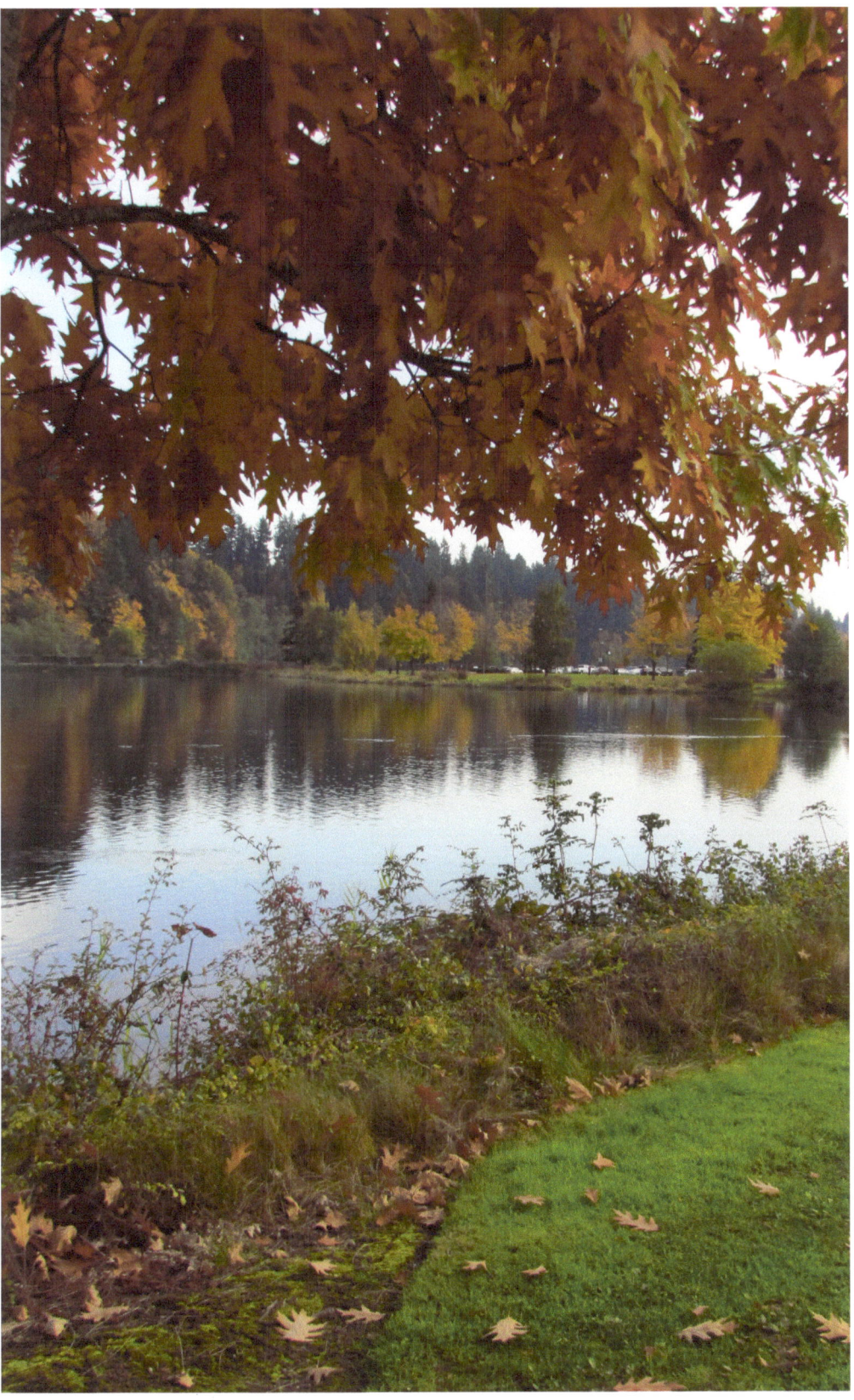

<u>FREE FORM AUTUMN 1</u>

Autumn is:
Wisps of wood stove smoke curling through the air,
The warmth of an evening fire contrasted against the cold,
Fireplaces casting a romantic orange glow,
Fog snuggled around the rivers and in the valleys,
A bright colored leaf floating down the stream,
The call of geese winging overhead in a "V,"
Natures call to hunker down and snuggle a little bit more.

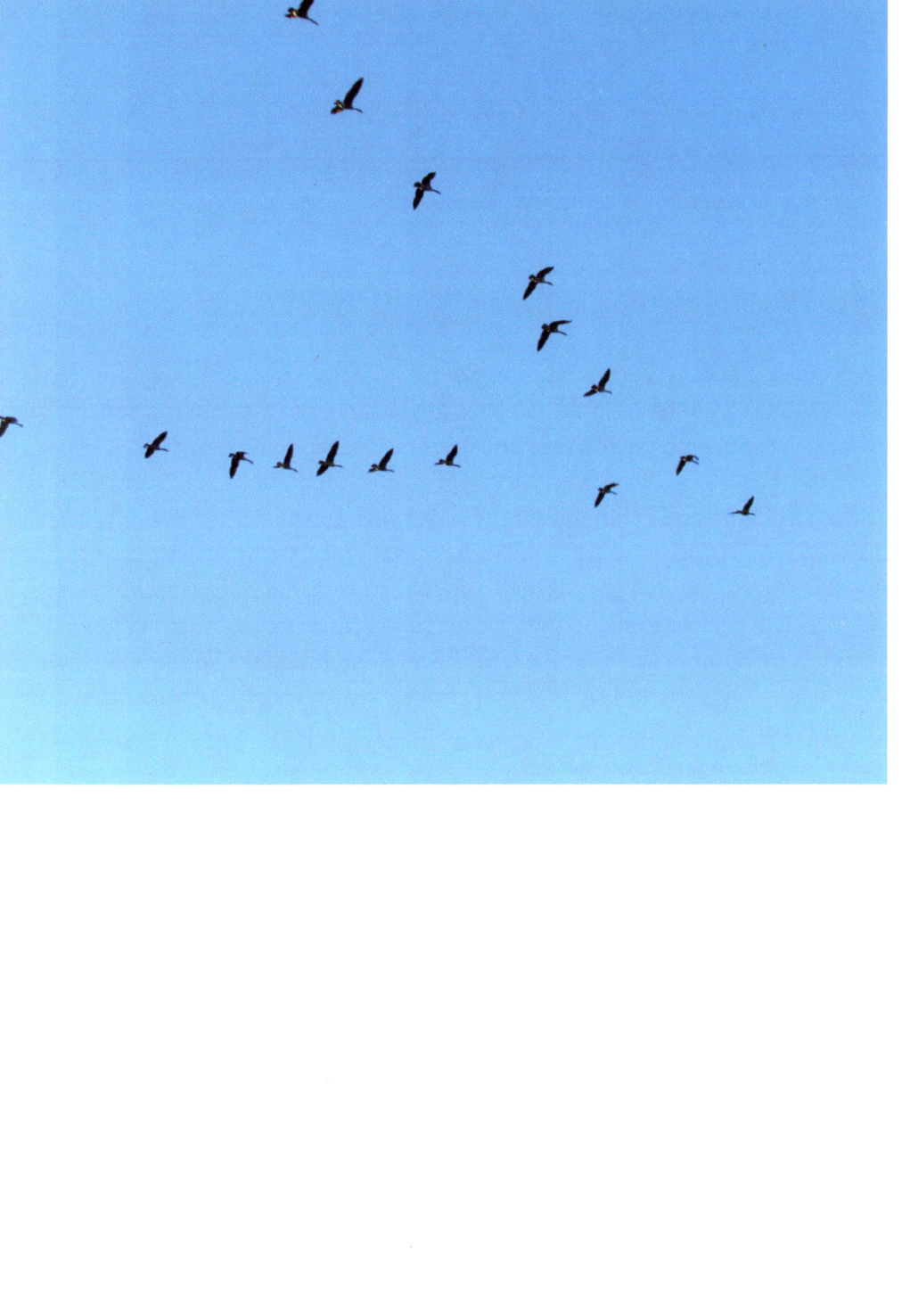

THOUGHTS

Autumn is a time of seeing inner beauty.

The vibrant colors and beauty that we see in the leaves comes from within. That beauty is already there we just do not see the beauty until the Autumn season. The browns, yellows, oranges and reds only become visible as the green fades.

Chlorophyll is green in color giving the leaves their green color. Chlorophyll is also vital for photosynthesis. Photosynthesis is a process that allows plants to absorb energy from sunlight. This also gives the plants their green appearance as the plant is reflecting more of the green light spectrum and absorbing more of the other spectrums. So, the green is very prevalent during the spring and summer as sunlight is converted to energy through photosynthesis. As the amount of sunlight decreases in Autumn and the photosynthesis process diminishes the other colors become evident and visible.

Isn't that like people? If you only look at the surface you do not see the inner beauty. Sometimes events cause us to look beyond the exterior and to see the inner colors and beauty. We can also foster a habit of looking at the inner beauty.

Facing Page: Capitol Lake, Olympia, Washington

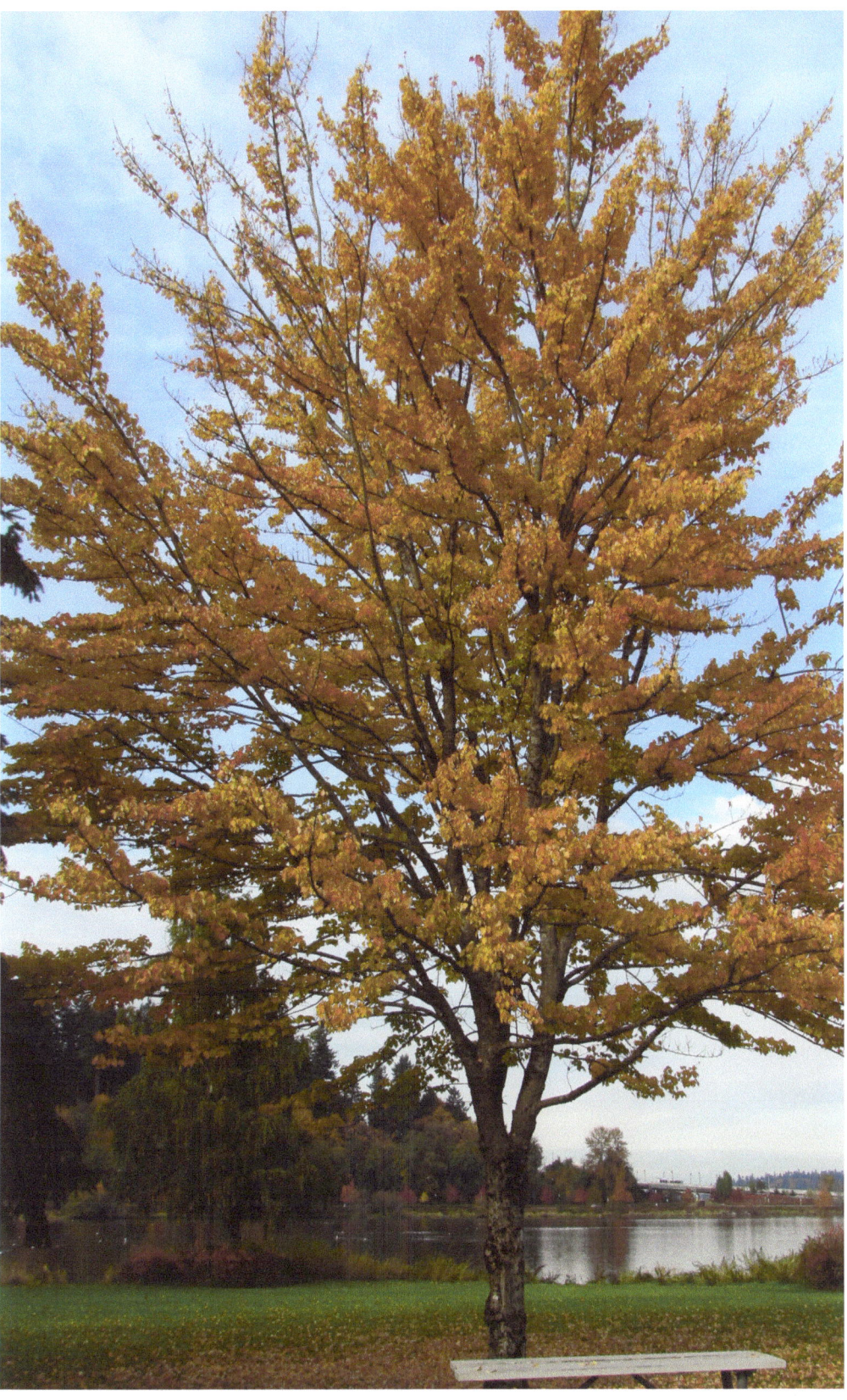

FREE FORM AUTUMN 2

Autumn is:
Crisp air,
Trees ablaze
Natures color show,
Warm days and cold nights,
A unique set of scents and smells.

Facing Page: Capitol Lake, Olympia, Washington

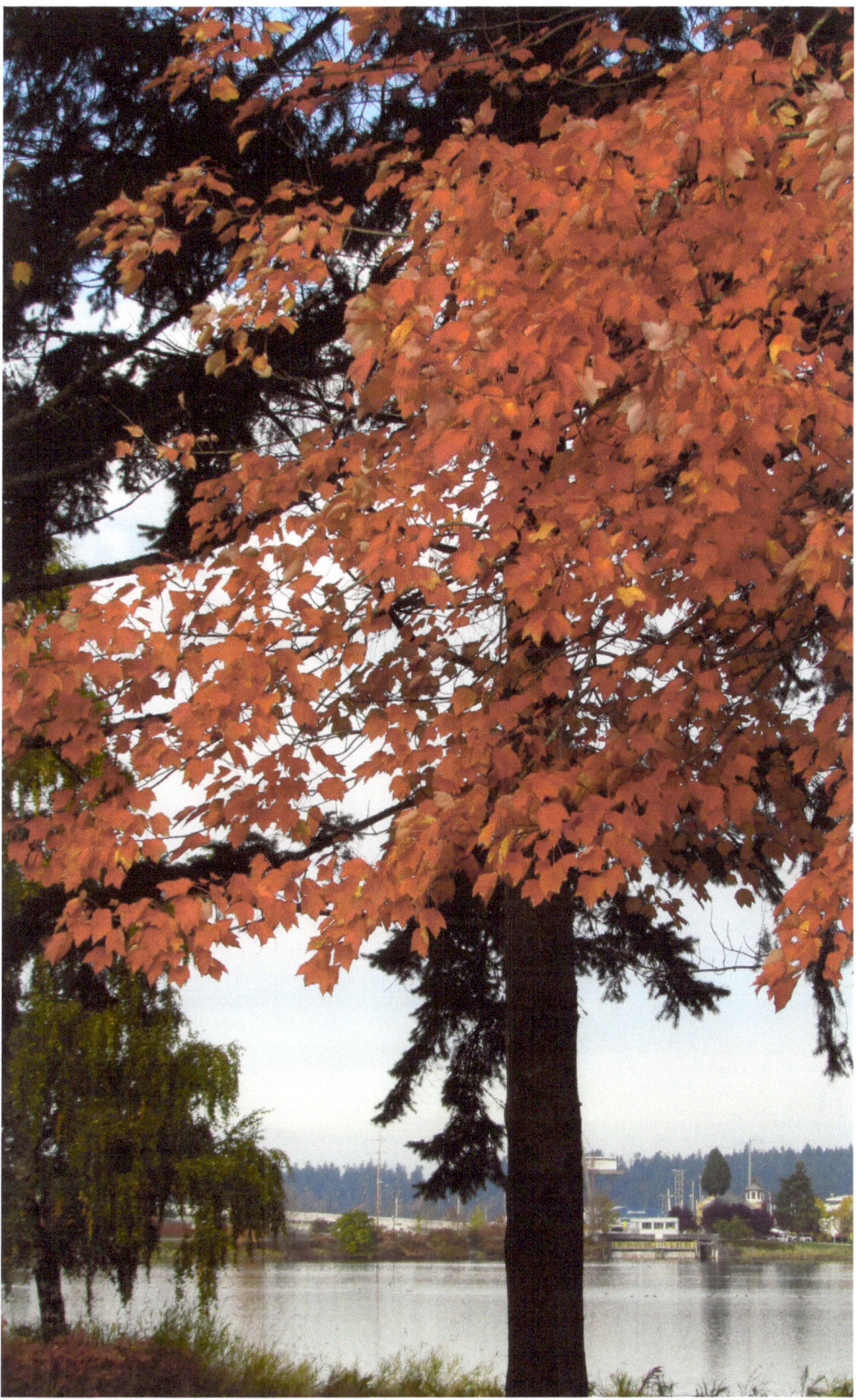

<u>FACTS</u>

In the process of photosynthesis trees pull water from the ground through their roots, take carbon dioxide from the air, and absorb energy from sunlight and from those ingredients produce sugar. The sugar is then a source of energy for the plant.

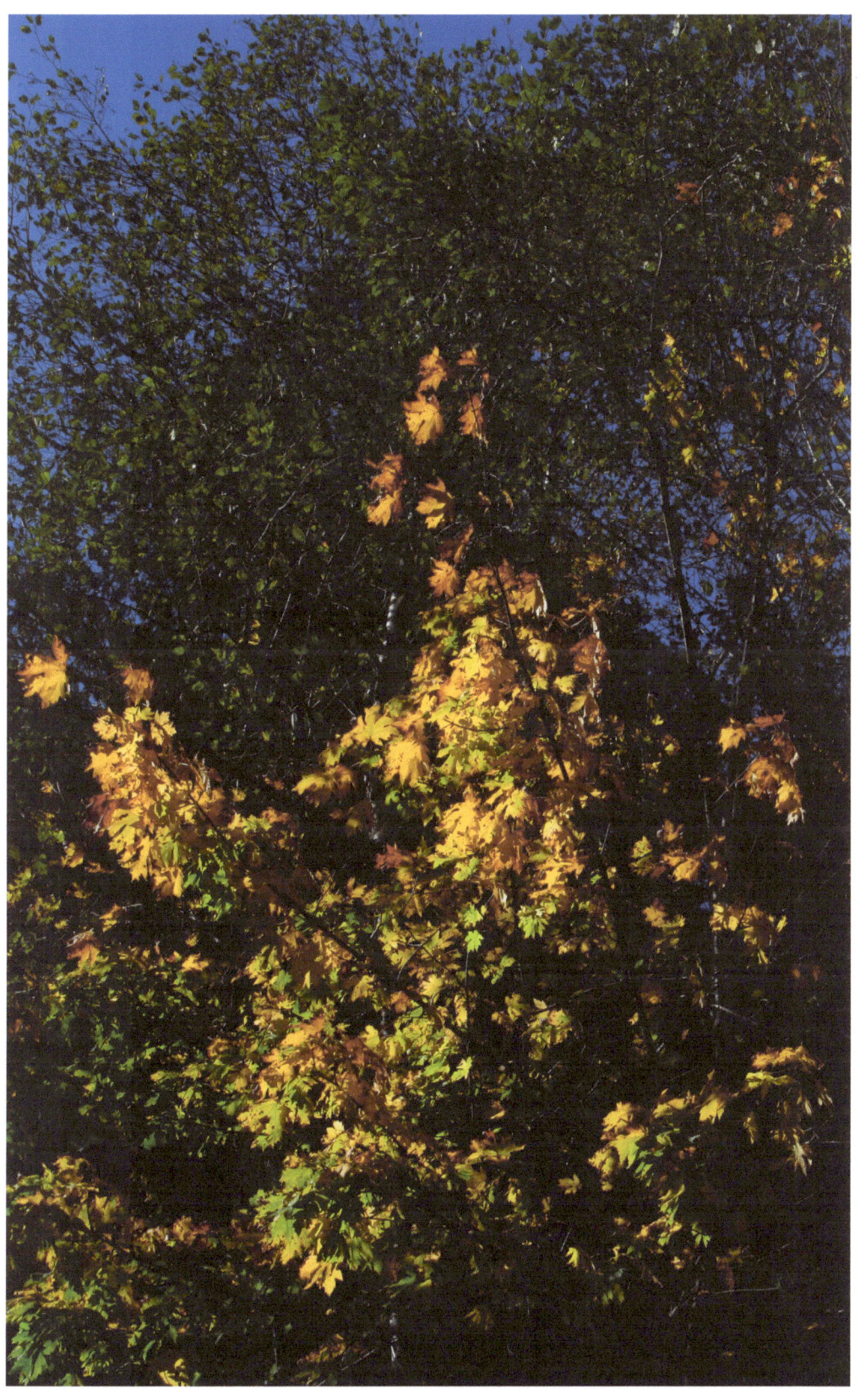

FACTS

Sugars and amino acids serve as a type of antifreeze for the plants.

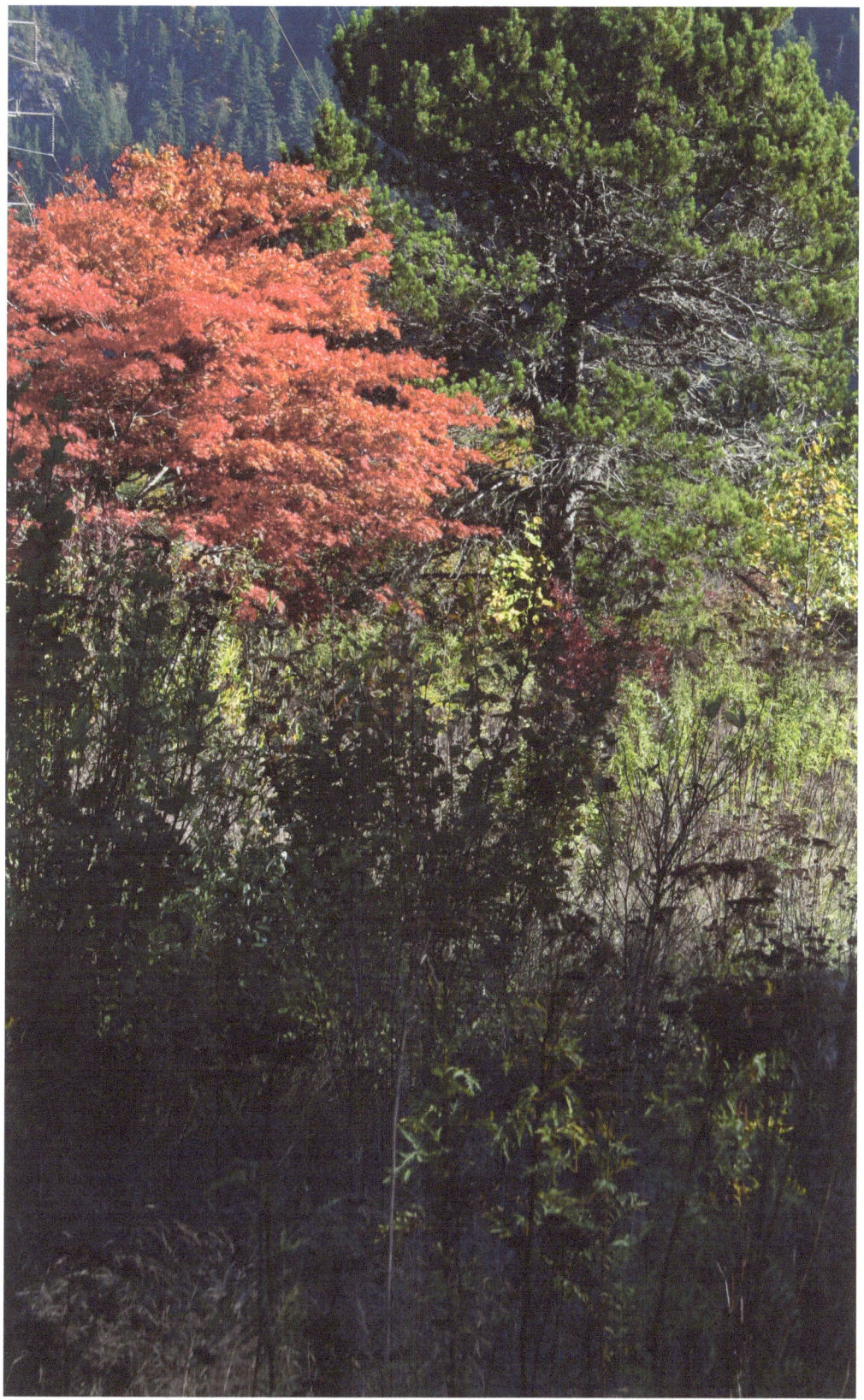

<u>FACTS</u>

Trees draw the nutrients from the leaves into the stems and roots before the leaves fall off. It is actually a very efficient process.

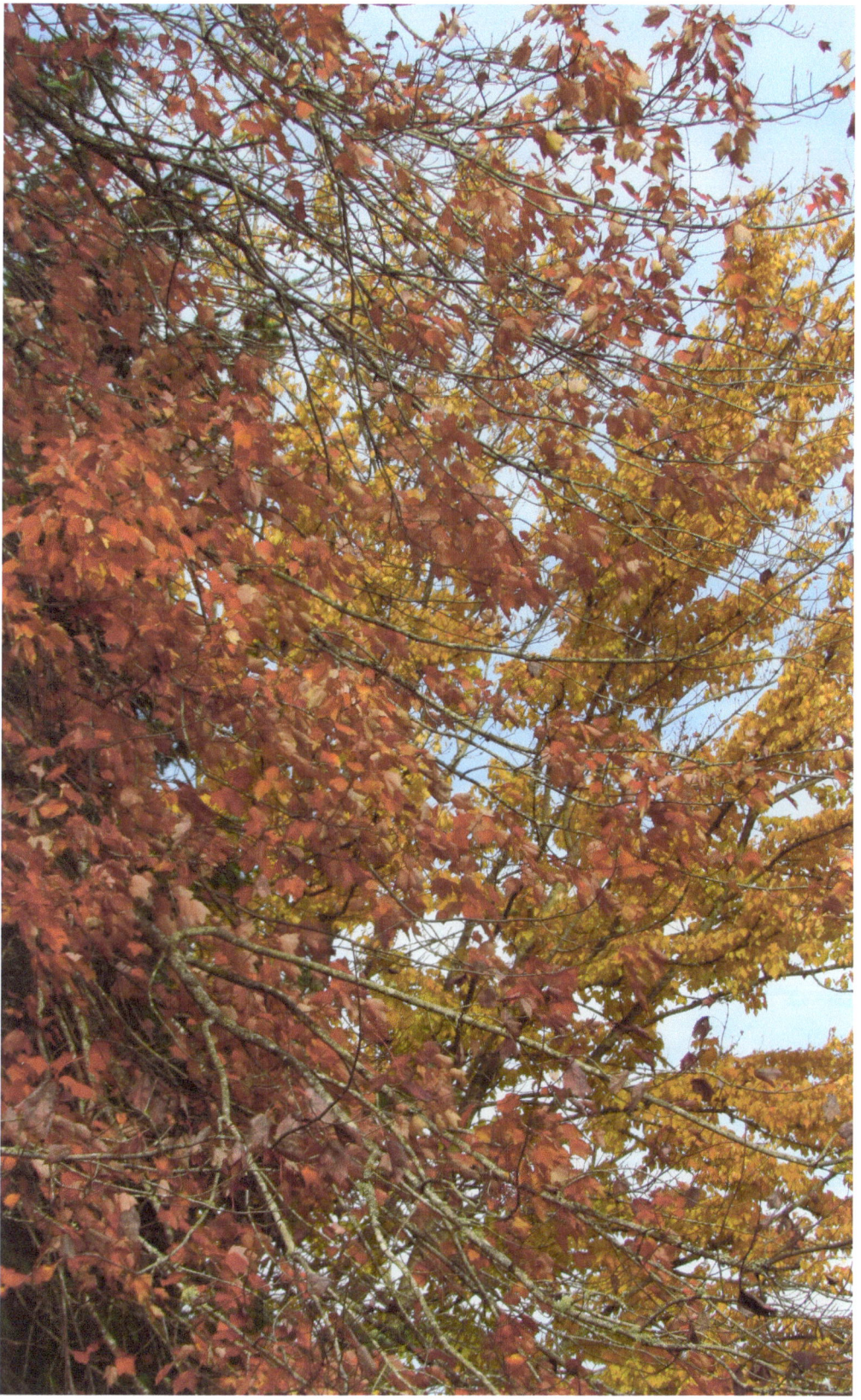

FACTS

Autumn colors are usually most vibrant in years that include:

* A warm and wet spring
* A decent summer
* An Autumn with warm sunny days and cool or cold nights, preferably 40 degrees or less.

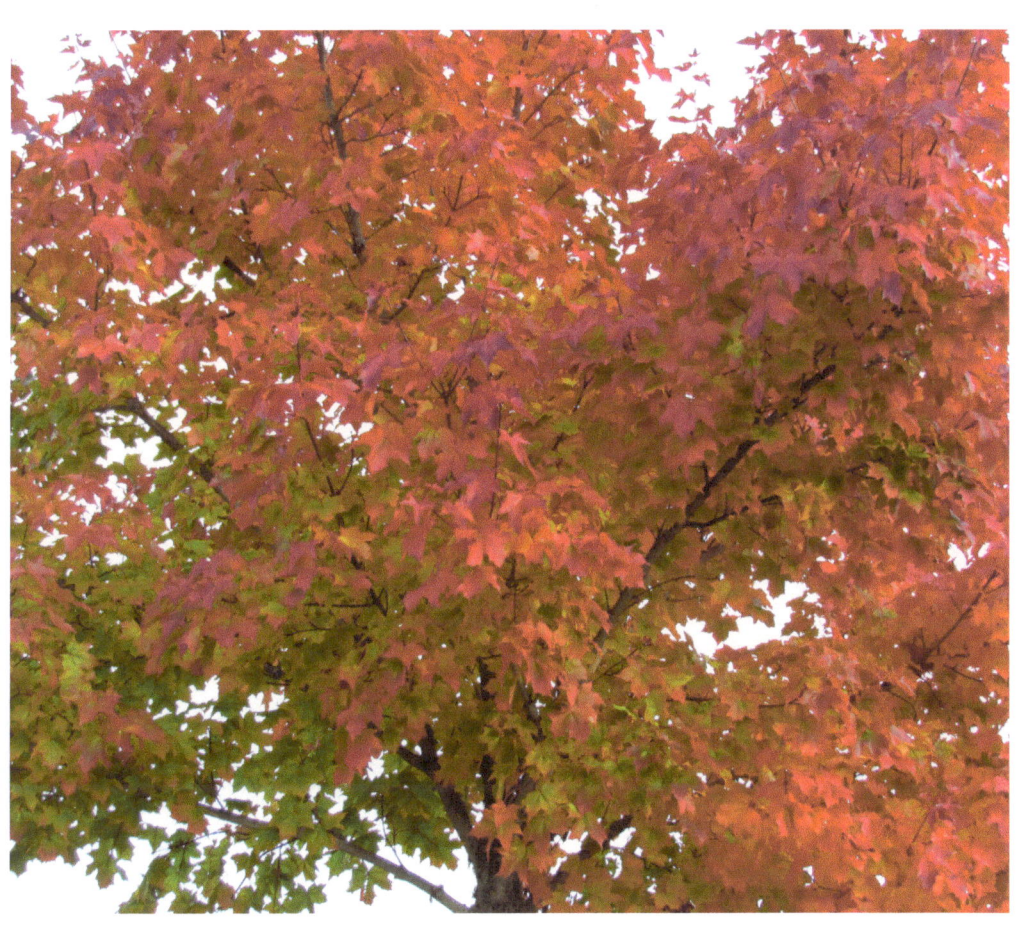

FACTS

There is some variation in what causes the Autumn colors but generally:
* Bright red and purple is caused by the presence of glucose
* Orange is caused by the presence of carotene
* Yellow is caused by the presence of xanthophyll (a carotenoid pigment)
* Brown is caused by the presence of tannin.

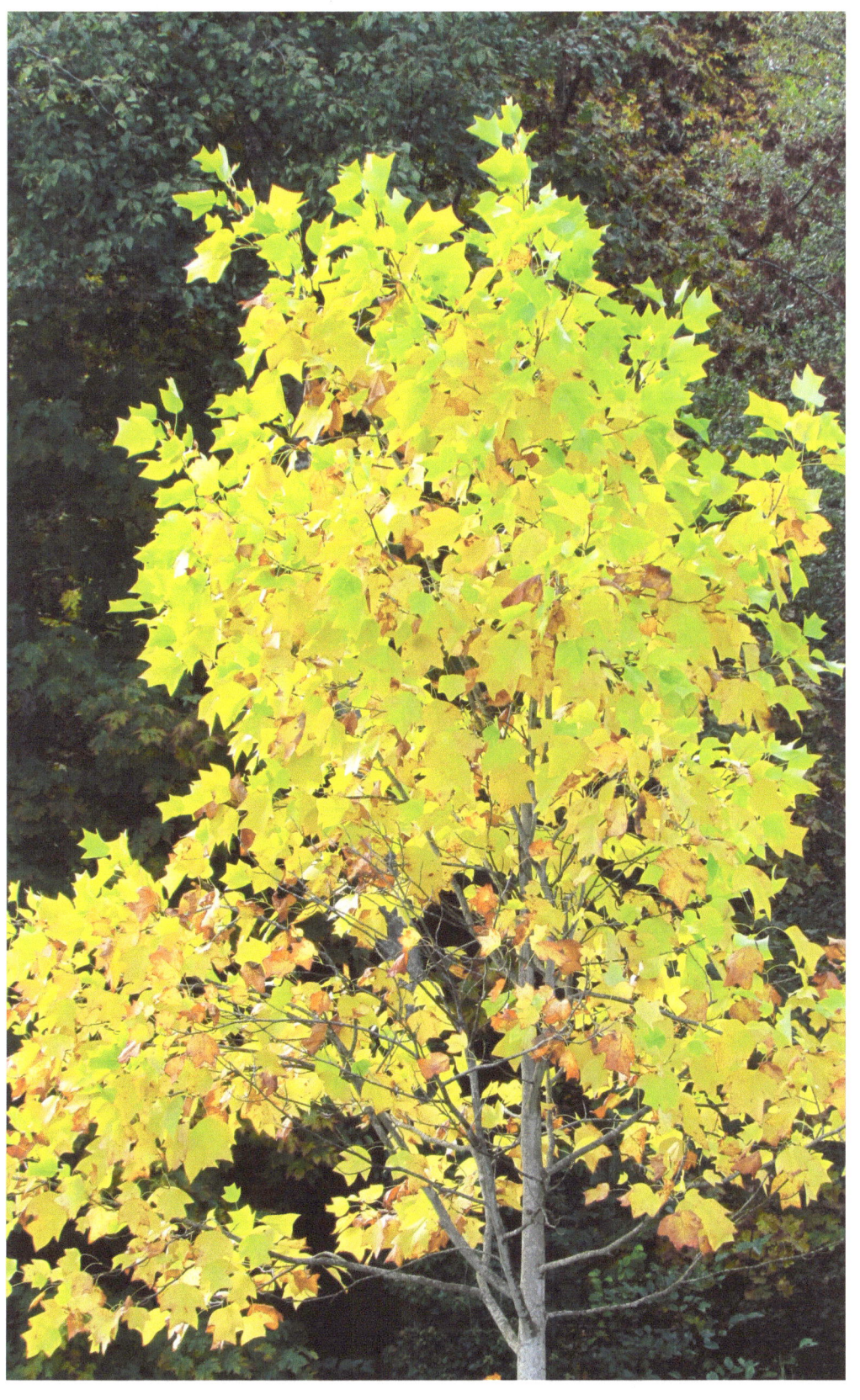

FACTS

Leaves can be a source of minerals for soil through mulching or composting.

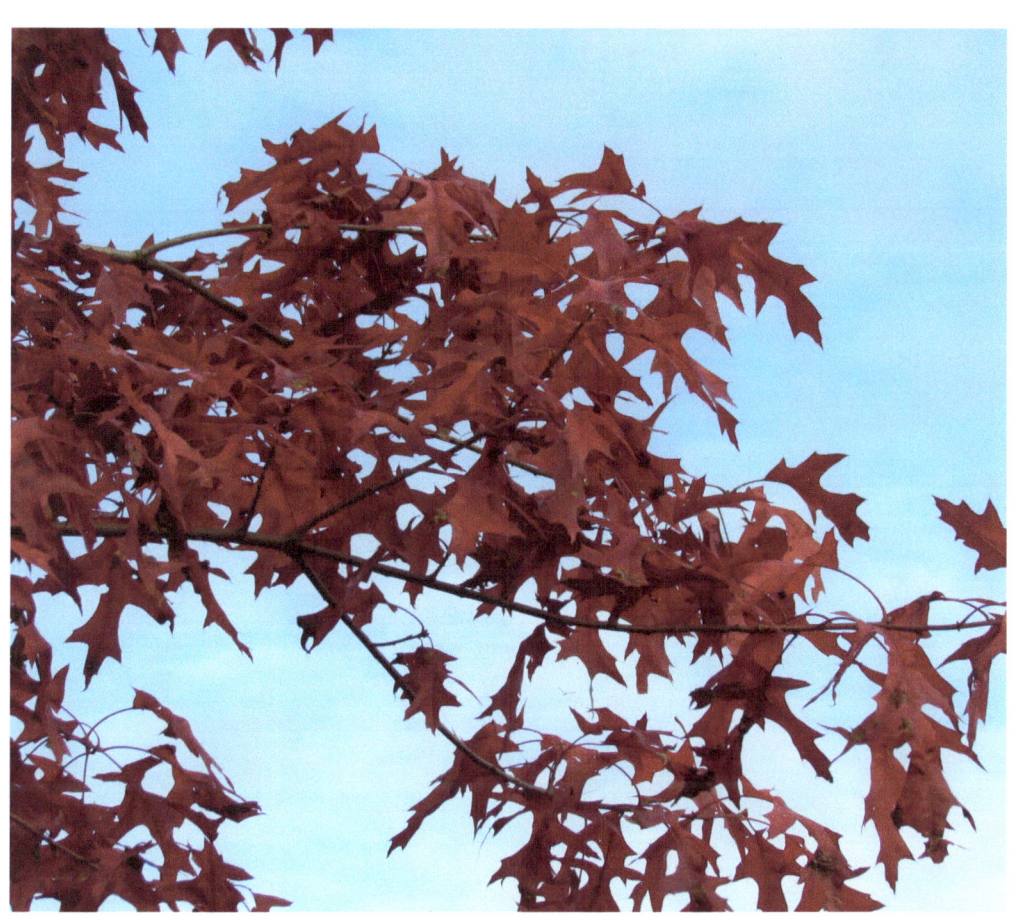

FACTS

An acre of trees:
* Produce 4,280 pounds of oxygen, enough for 18 people breathing for a year
* Produce 4,000 pounds of wood per year
* Consumes as much carbon dioxide as is produced by 26,000 miles of driving or about 5,880 pounds.

A single tree produces enough oxygen for two people.

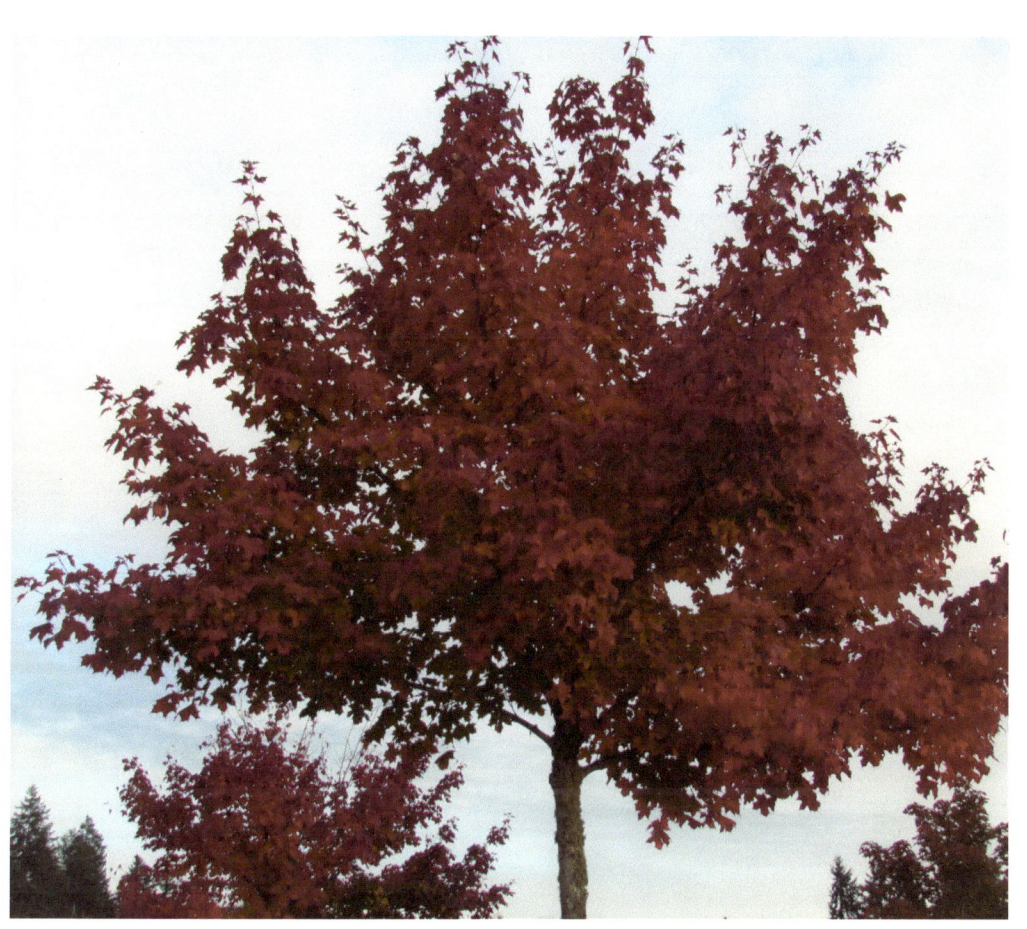

FACTS

Autumn celebrations include:
  * Harvest festivals
  * Octoberfests
  * Halloween / All Saints Day
  * Thanksgiving
  * Fall equinox
  * Moon Festival in China
  * Yom Kippur
  * Rosh Hashanah (Jewish new year)
  * Chanukah (Jewish).

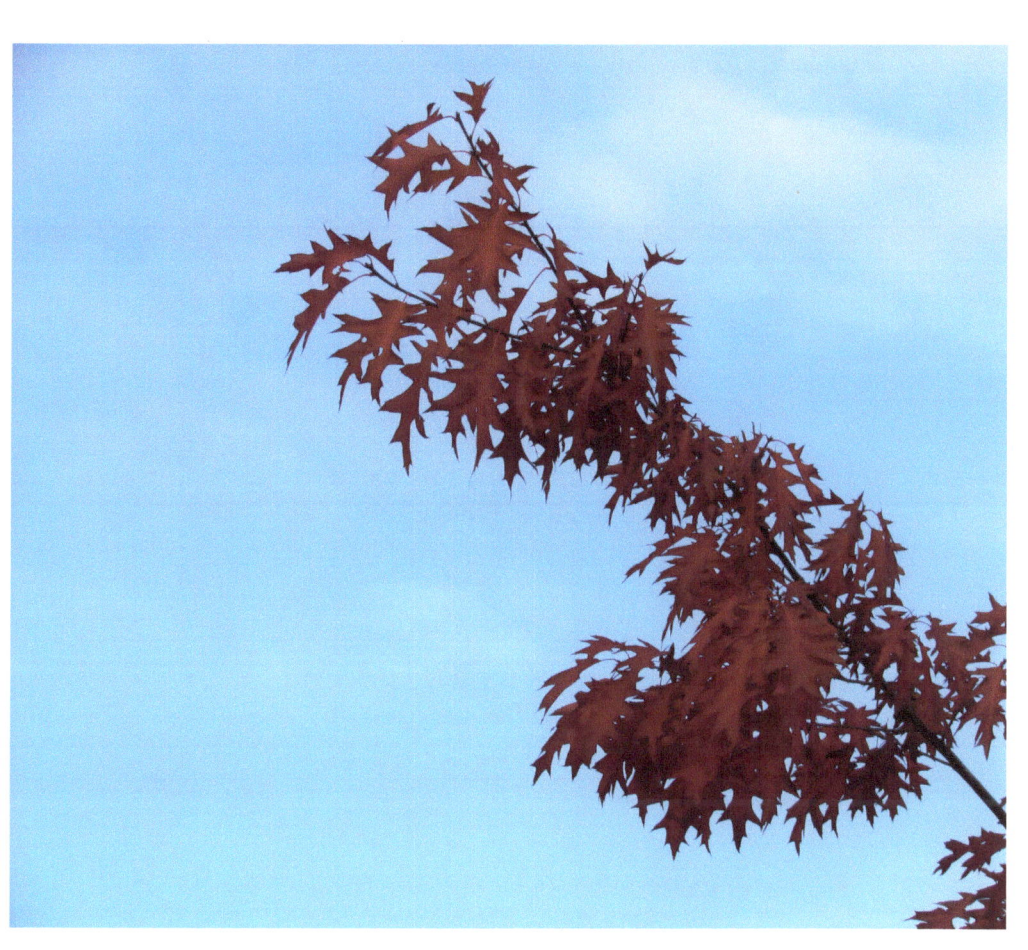

AUTUMN ACTIVITIES

Raking piles of leaves
Running through the leaves
Taking crisp morning walks
Basking in the warm afternoon sun
Taking a cool evening stroll
Drives to see the colors
Family and friends in for the evening
Sipping a warm drink
Settling in with a good book
Snuggling in front of the fire

Facing Page: Capitol Lake, Olympia, Washington

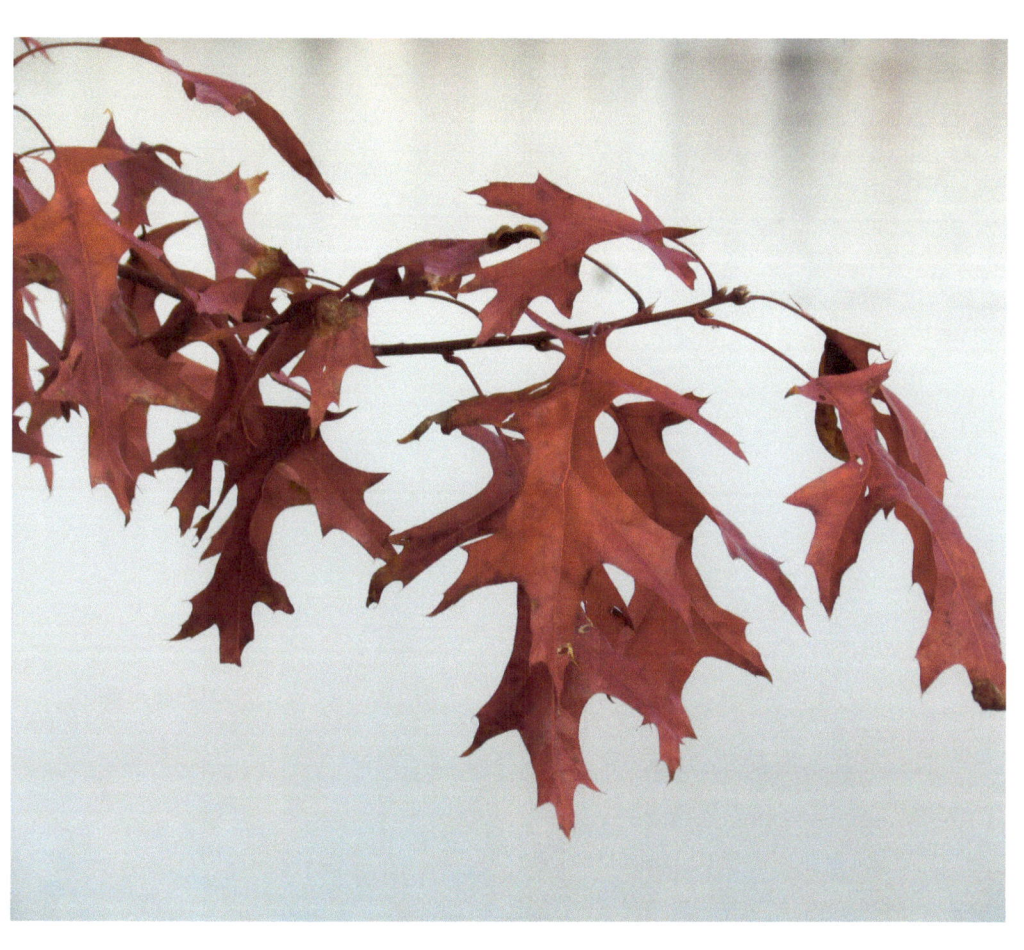

FACTS

Animals that hibernate or mostly sleep through winter

Warm Blooded

Badgers

Bats

Bears

Dormouse

Groundhogs or Woodchucks

Hedgehogs

Prairie Dogs

Raccoons

Skunks

Squirrels & Chipmunks

Cold Blooded

Bees

Earthworms

Frogs & Toads

Lizards

Moths

Snakes

Animals that migrate

African Elephant

Arctic Tern

Butterflies

Caribou

Ducks

Elk

Geese

Gnu

Japanese Beetle

Moths

Reindeer

Termites

Whales

Wildebeest

Facing Page: Capitol Lake, Olympia, Washington

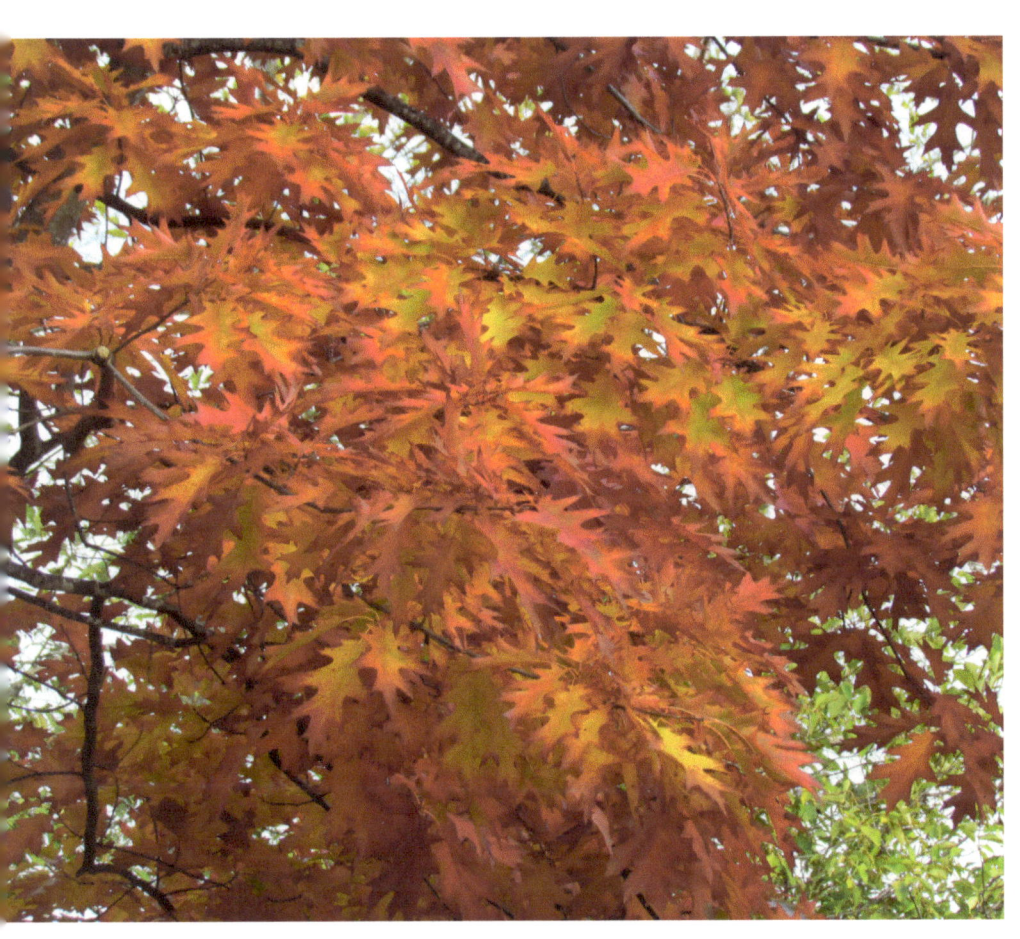

<u>AUTUMN TERSE VERSE 1</u>

Leaves crunching
Apple munching
Colors bright
Migratory flight
Fog shrouded
Sky clouded
Azure sky
Pumpkin pie
Harvest moon
Final prune
Frosty shroud
Shivering crowd
Spun cocoon
Winter soon

Facing Page: Capitol Lake, Olympia, Washington

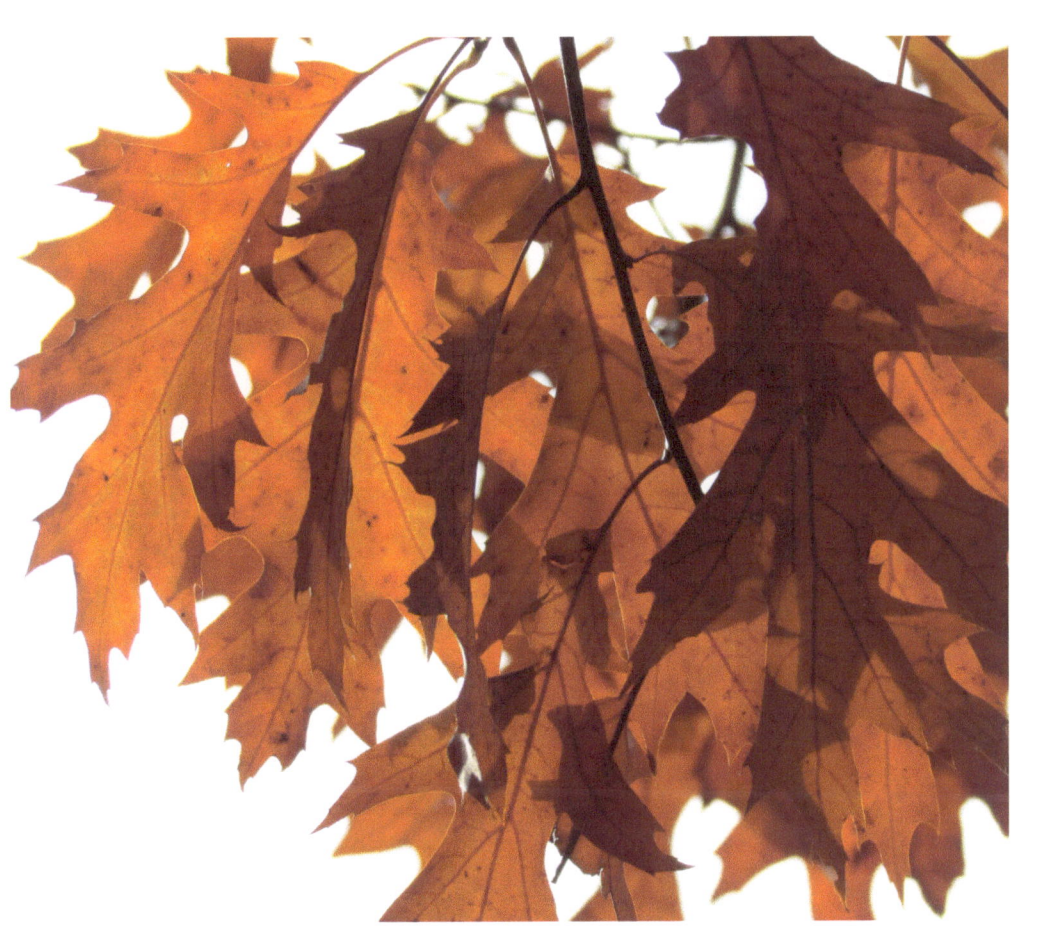

FREE FORM AUTUMN 3

Autumn is:
Harvesting done,
Slowing down,
Reflecting more.

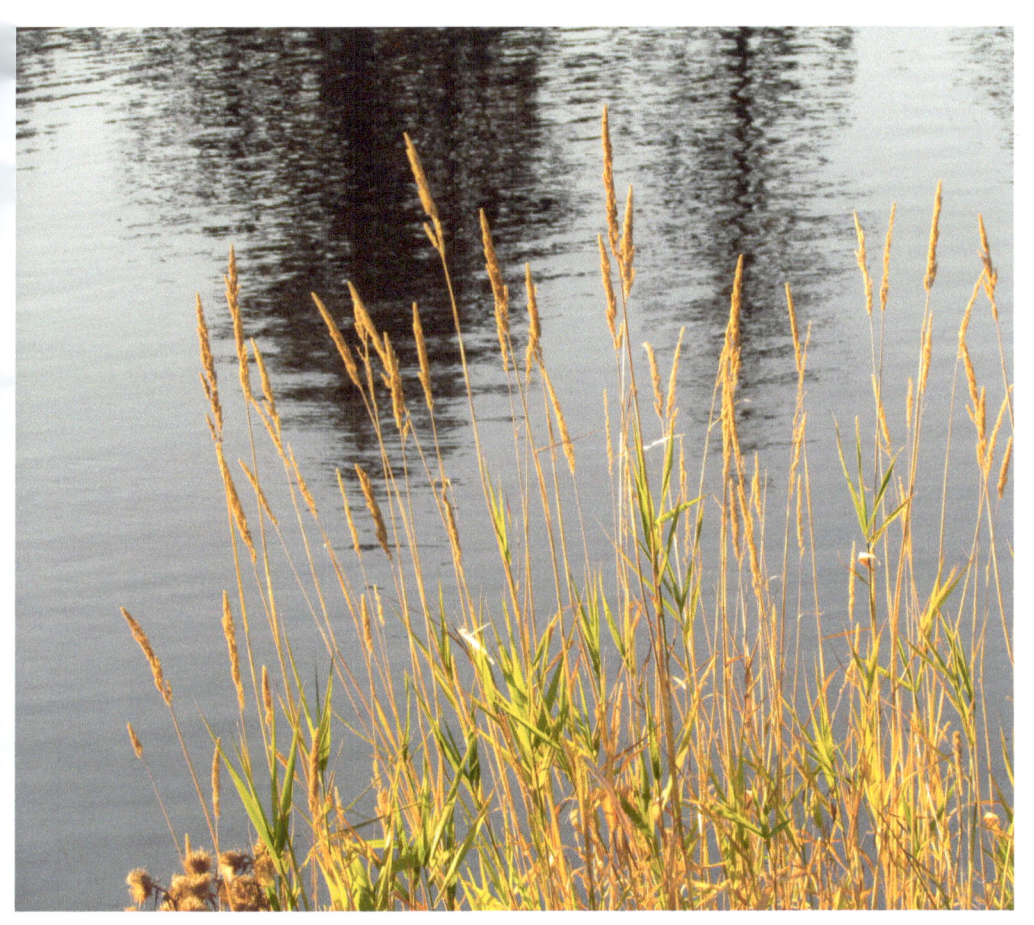

THOUGHTS

Autumn is the season that prepares us for and transitions us, and the rest of nature as well, into winter.

For most of human existence we have lived in harmony with natures rhythms. Many people have lost at least some of that blessing.

It is worth striving to sense the created rhythms, to learn the lessons that they have for us, to embrace them and celebrate them, to see how in tune with the created rhythms we can become.